Being a Good Citizen

Way to Be!

A Book About Citizenship

by Mary Small   illustrated by Stacey Previn

PICTURE WINDOW BOOKS
Minneapolis, Minnesota

Thanks to our advisers for their expertise, research, and advice:

Bambi L. Wagner, Director of Education
Institute for Character Development, Des Moines, Iowa
National Faculty Member/ Trainer,
Josephson Institute of Ethics - CHARACTER COUNTS!sm
Los Angeles, California

Susan Kesselring, M.A., Literacy Educator
Rosemount-Apple Valley-Eagan (Minnesota) School District

Editorial Director: Carol Jones
Managing Editor: Catherine Neitge
Creative Director: Keith Griffin
Editor: Jacqueline A. Wolfe
Story Consultant: Terry Flaherty
Designer: Joe Anderson
Page Production: Picture Window Books
The illustrations in this book were created with acrylics.

Picture Window Books
1710 Roe Crest Drive
North Mankato, MN 56003
www.capstonepub.com

Library of Congress Cataloging-in-Publication Data
Small, Mary.
Being a good citizen / by Mary Small ; illustrated by Stacey Previn.
p. cm. – (Way to be!)
Includes bibliographical references and index.
ISBN 978-1-4048-1050-1 (library binding)
ISBN 978-1-4048-1785-2 (paperback)
1. Citizenship—Juvenile literature. I. Previn, Stacey, ill. II. Title. III. Series.
JF801.S548 2006
323.6'5–dc22   2005004273

Printed in the United States of America in North Mankato, Minnesota.
082017   010708R

Living in a country is like being part of a big, special club. You are a member of that club every day. If your club is going to be a success, every member has to help. Being a good citizen means you are helping your country be the best it can be.

There are lots of ways to be a good citizen.

Joe knows the lakes need to be cleaner,
so he speaks out against pollution.

He is being a good citizen.

Kelly helps shovel her neighbor's sidewalk after it snows.

She is being a good citizen.

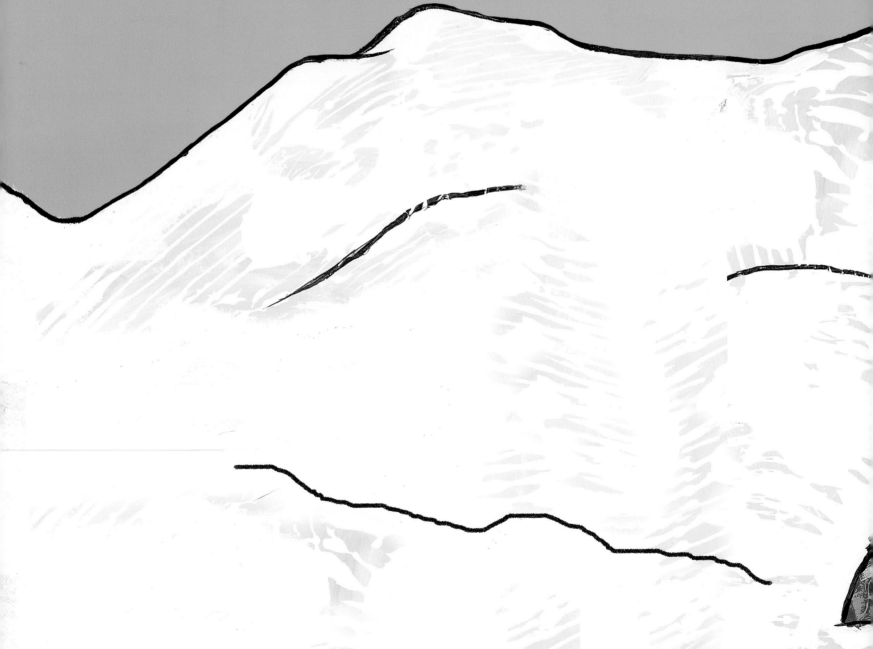

When a new family moves to town, the children from the neighborhood stop by to say hello.

They are being good citizens.

When water spills on the basketball court,
Mary quickly wipes it up so no one will slip.

She is being a good citizen.

12

Stacy picks up the trash from the ground and throws it away even though it is not hers.

She is being a good citizen.

Voting for local and state officials is very important. Jimmy wakes his parents up bright and early on election day to make sure they don't forget!

He is being a good citizen.

Mrs. Jones and her students study the history of their country.

They are being good citizens.

18

Jenna works as a crossing guard to help keep people and animals safe.

She is being a good citizen.

Josh protects the small and weak from harm.

He is being a good citizen.

Ms. Marcy and Samantha plant flowers to make the neighborhood a more colorful place.

They are being good citizens.

More Books to Read

Hagler, Linda D. Good *Citizenship Counts*. Chapin, S.D.: YouthLight, 2003.

Loewen, Nancy. *We Live Here Too! : Kids Talk About Good Citizenship*. Minneapolis: Picture Window Books, 2003.

Riehecky, Janet. *Citizenship*. Mankato, Minn.: Capstone Press, 2005.

On the Web

FactHound offers a safe, fun way to find Web sites related to topics in this book. All of the sites on FactHound have been researched by our staff.

1. Visit www.facthound.com
2. Type in this special code: 1404810501
3. Click the Fetch It button.

Your trusty FactHound will fetch the best Web sites for you!

Index

Look for all of the books in the Way to Be! series:

Being a Good Citizen

Being Brave

Being Considerate

Being Cooperative

Being Courageous

Being Fair

Being Honest

Being Respectful

Being Responsible

Being Tolerant

Being Trustworthy

Caring

Manners at School

Manners at the Table

Manners in Public

Manners in the Library

Manners on the Playground

Manners on the Telephone